This book about

Brave David

belongs to

· ·

LION
CHILDREN'S

When he was very little, David liked
to throw stones.

When he was bigger, he learned
to throw them with
a sling.

He was good
at throwing – he
could hit what
he wanted.

At night, his mother told him
about God.

She taught him to say
thank-you prayers to God
for everything he had
and for all the things
he could do.

When David was a bit older,
his job was looking after
the sheep.

He threw stones to scare
away wild animals.

David was never scared. He sang
thank-you songs to God for
everything he had and
for all the things he
could do.

One day, David went to visit his big
brothers. They were soldiers.

They were fighting fierce
enemies.

One was a giant.
He wore shiny battle
clothes and had a
big spear. "I am
Goliath," roared the
giant. "If anyone can
beat me, then my
army will go away!
Who dares to try?"

"I dare," said David. For David
believed that God was always
with him and would help
him win.

"You're too little,"
said his brothers.

"You're too little,"
said his king.

"But I can fight lions and bears and wolves, and I know God is with me," said David.

"Take care," they warned.

David went out.

He picked up
five stones.

"How dare you fight
me like that!" said
the giant.

"I dare because God is with me,"
said David. He put a stone in his sling.

He threw.

The giant fell.

David grew up to be the next king
of his people. He still sang thank-you
songs to God for everything he had
and for all he could do.

"Dear God, you are my shepherd,
You give me all I need –
My food, my drink, a place to rest,
Yes, you are good indeed.
When all the world seems gloomy
And scary things are near,
You always take good care of me
And so I need not fear.
You've given me so many things,
And everyone can see
The special loving kindness
You always show to me."

Special Words

dare to risk doing something dangerous

giant someone who is unusually tall

prayer talking and listening to God

shepherd someone who looks after sheep

sling a pocket-on-a-string for throwing stones

soldier someone who fights a war

A Prayer

Thank you, dear God,
for the good things I have,
and for all of the things I can do.
Help me to use them
with care and with love
today, and my whole life through.

Text by Lois Rock
Illustrations copyright © 2003 Alex Ayliffe
This edition copyright © 2011 Lion Hudson

The moral rights of the author and illustrator
have been asserted

A Lion Children's Book
an imprint of
Lion Hudson plc
Wilkinson House, Jordan Hill Road,
Oxford OX2 8DR, England
www.lionhudson.com
ISBN 978 0 7459 6307 5

First edition 2008
This edition 2011
10 9 8 7 6 5 4 3 2 1

A catalogue record for this book is available
from the British Library

Typeset in 13/16 Baskerville
Printed in China November 2011 (manufacturer LH06)